ideals
COUNTRYSIDE

Gray pearly dawn, ending of night,
The coming day tipped with golden light,
New promises with morning sun,
Hushed silence ere the day's begun,
Soft misty shadows, morning dew,
Deep haze of fog while day is new...
This is the beauty of the countryside.

Mamie Ozburn Odum

ISBN 0-8249-1052-4

Publisher, Patricia A. Pingry
Editor, Ramona Richards
Art Director, David Lenz
Production Manager, Jan Johnson
Permissions, Kathleen Gilbert
Copy Editor, Peggy Schaefer
Typesetter, Karen Davidson

Front and back covers from H. Armstrong Roberts

Inside front cover from Grant Heilman Photography
Inside back cover by Ed Cooper

IDEALS—Vol. 44, No. 4, June MCMLXXXVII IDEALS (ISSN 0019-137X) is published eight times a year,
February, March, May, June, August, September, November, December
by IDEALS PUBLISHING CORPORATION, Nelson Place at Elm Hill Pike, Nashville, Tenn. 37214-8000
Second class postage paid at Nashville, Tennessee, and additional mailing offices.
Copyright © MCMLXXXVII by IDEALS PUBLISHING CORPORATION.
POSTMASTER: Send address changes to Ideals, Post Office Box 148000, Nashville, Tenn. 37214-8000
All rights reserved. Title IDEALS registered U.S. Patent Office.
Published simultaneously in Canada.

SINGLE ISSUE—$3.50
ONE-YEAR SUBSCRIPTION—eight consecutive issues as published—$15.95
TWO-YEAR SUBSCRIPTION—sixteen consecutive issues as published—$27.95
Outside U.S.A., add $4.00 per subscription year for postage and handling.

A Country Garden

I find a country garden
Is the sweetest one of all,
With ragged roses climbing
Along a garden wall.
Forget-me-nots and daisies
All do their own sweet part
To bring a touch of heaven
To a corner of my heart.

I find a country garden
Quite the loveliest by far.
It brings a quiet beauty
No matter where you are;
It soothes the tired spirit
And puts the heart at rest.
A quiet country garden
Is by far the loveliest.

Carice Williams

Country Chronicle

June ushers in some of the most delightful days of the year. With her arrival, a summer steadiness replaces the inconsistencies of late frosts and chilling rains, fulfilling spring's promise of golden days and fields of green.

Having lived for many years on a small farm in upstate New York, I knew well the certainty of June. Gone was the hesitation of the earlier season. When the timothy grew tall enough to undulate in the wind and the daisies and hawkweed, sorrel and Queen Anne's lace joined the procession of blooms, there remained no doubt that the wild strawberry would soon be ripening

in old, neglected fields. The strawberry thrived even in fields which had not seen a plow or mowing machine in years.

One of my favorite berry fields was located just beyond our pasture wall, a place I visited often. To get there, I would cross the creek where the turbulence of waters from centuries past had carved a channel through layers of rocks and stone. I would pass wild roses on a pasture ledge where the killdeer had a nest among the fragments of lichened stones. I would walk through the steeple bush in the bog where, on an April evening, I had watched and listened as the woodcock went through its flight song.

Once in the field, I could detect the location of the ripened fruit merely by the fragrance that filled the air. It was rich and sweet, tempting and tantalizing. There I picked strawberries as I listened to the rollicking song of the bobolink and the chatter of barn swallows as they swooped and dived over the flat.

There, in the wild strawberry field, I came to know the intimacy and companionship of the land. There I came to know of June and her fulfillment of promises.

Lansing Christman

Journey's End

This morning, when I awoke, the air was cool;
The shadows still were long and deep
Upon the grass where dewdrops clung,
Loathe to part company with such a fine companion
As the summer night.

I sighed to see the freshness of the morning
Surrender to the heat of noonday sun;
And longingly, I wondered why
The whole of day could not be cool and sweet
As is the early morn.

Yet, would not one regret missing the glory
Of a glowing sunset at close of day,
The brilliance of starlight and the beauty
Of a waning moon, the peacefulness
That comes at eventide?

When the flush of youth is on our cheeks,
We think we should like to keep it so;
But glorious sunsets and the light of distant stars
Belong to the night and are only found
At journey's end.

Edna Bacon Morrison

Readers'

Clothesline

On every farm they used to hang on Mondays—
shirttails, towels, and overalls.
Tucked on the last line, out of sight,
long johns floundered helplessly, upside down,
and socks wriggled pinched toes.
Some dresses waited solemn and taut
on measured lines tied to neat poles.
Others tumbled sloppily from apple branches,
teasing the leaves.

On every farm on summer Monday mornings, children hid,
sweetly buffeted between blanket and sheet
or, lying in grass, watched from below
the slow rising to wind and snap-flap down.
They sang secrets.

On every farm in winter, Monday's clothes stood rigid—
rebels staying out all night, stiff and silent
under a cold, white moon,
listening to the huddled collies' cry.
At dazzled day, snatched from an icy clutch
and mellowed by light,
they spent the afternoon at kitchen's stove,
gossiping on wooden racks.

On every Monday morning's farm, clotheslines have fallen.
Who now will watch over the winter moon—
who, leap billowing into summer's noon?

Jean Z. Liebenthal
Idaho Falls, Idaho

Editor's Note: Readers are invited to submit unpublished, original poetry, short anecdotes, and humorous reflections on life for possible publication in future I*deals* issues. Please send copies only; manuscripts will not be returned. Writers will receive $10 for each published submission. Send materials to "Readers' Reflections," Ideals Publishing Corporation, Nelson Place at Elm Hill Pike, Nashville, Tennessee 37214.

Reflections

Summer's Gifts

Hooped little green worms, measuring inches,
Fast golden darts of sun-splashed finches,
Cicadas tuning their rusty old fiddles,
Dark clouds churning weathermen's riddles.

Hummingbirds searching through velvety roses,
Gold buttercup smudges on upturned noses,
Blueberries plunking in Grandma's tin pail,
Wild vines tugging the ancient split rail.

Porch swings creaking in heat of midday,
Voices of children involved in their play,
Sharp knives of lightning slicing the sky,
Dizzy old windmills whirling so high.

Summer sneaks in between tulips and clover;
She stays but awhile, her days are soon over.
Take time to accept the gifts that she brings;
You'll find she is laden with so many things.

Dawn Corkins
Hudsonville, Michigan

Cathedral of the Smokies

The Cathedral of the Smokies,
Where I worship with my friends,
Offers inspiration daily,
Music furnished by the winds.

Portals formed by massive hemlocks,
Emerald ceilings hung with grace,
Sounds of birdsong break the silence;
Surely God is in this place.

There's just enough of Eden's touch
To stir our minds with misty dream.
We drink our fill of nature's plenty,
Baptized in an icy stream.

Yes, I'm impressed by man's obsession—
I've seen the spires of Notre Dame,
But my Cathedral of the Smokies
Puts the best of man to shame.

Ron Evans
Corbin, Kentucky

Summertime

If you'll follow the country lane at will
To wherever it leads beyond the hill,
Around the turn and past the pines,
You'll find the scenes of summertime.

There is the splash of a noisy stream,
A flash of color from birds on wing,
The darting motion of a dragonfly
Playing his game of search and spy.

The inviting reach of a shady tree
Offers the hum of honeybees,
While above, the restless, rustling leaves
Whisper a secret to the gentle breeze.

The wind lightly kisses the children at play
And in perfect tune with the summer day,
Sweeps over the meadow, setting flowers in motion
Like constant waves on a golden ocean.

And morning glories grow in shades of blue,
Holding diamonds of morning dew;
While a fluffy cloud chases the sun,
Racing the sunlight, and if it has won,

Other clouds darken and begin to glower,
Send pelting drops in a sudden rain shower.
When the rainstorm has gone, the sun shows its face
As if to atone for losing the race.

These words tell of summers I'll never forget,
A partial description of summer, but yet,
Mere words can but in part define
The enchanting ways of summertime.

Lucy E. Russell

Photo Opposite
MOUNTAIN WATERFALL
Dick Smith

AMERICAN CROSSROADS

Editor's Note: "American Crossroads" is a regular feature of *Ideals*, presenting photographs, stories, and jokes which have been submitted by our readers, about uniquely American events or experiences. If you have a 50 to 75 word account or photograph of an unusual or interesting occurrence unique to an American lifestyle or heritage, we would like to know. Send your submission to "American Crossroads," c/o Ideals Editorial, P.O. Box 141000, Nashville, TN 37214-1000. Please send only copies of manuscripts and duplicates of photographs or slides since submissions will not be returned. We will pay $10 for each printed submission.

"Waterball Fight," said the poster in the small town restaurant. I decided to stay and find out what it was all about.

There was a steel cable strung down the center of the street—on it ran a steel ball on a trolley. Below were teams of volunteer firemen who blasted the ball from opposite sides with their nozzles until it was pushed across one team's goal—a tug-of-war in reverse!

The wildly gyrating ball over their heads went back and forth, while the spray drenched contestants and spectators alike. Youngsters splashed happily in the puddles. It was as American as baseball and something you will never see in the big city.

Paul D. Jepson
Kirkland, Washington

More than fifty cowboy poets, artists, and craftsmen gathered in Alpine, Texas, on March 6 and 7, for the First Annual Texas Cowboy Poetry Gathering.

Inspired by the annual Cowboy Poetry Gatherings in Elko, Nevada, the Texas gathering was organized to spread the word that cowboy poetry and craftsmanship are the folk art of America's western heritage.

The two-day event featured cowboys, ranchers, and ranch wives reciting traditional and original poetry depicting the life and philosophy of the West. In addition, cowboy music, dancing, and public speaking were highlighted.

The grand finale of the Saturday night performance was the appearance of Tom Blasingame, a full-time working cowboy. While Red Steagall sang a song about Blasingame, the rest of the cast filed onstage and tipped their hats in his honor. Considered a living Texas legend by many cowboys, Blasingame served as wagon boss for two of Texas' famous old ranches, and at 89, he still breaks his own colts and loads his own feed.

Barney Nelson
Alpine, Texas

Don Edwards, cowboy balladeer and rancher

In the rural South, we have what is known as a "dinner on the ground." During the summer, many churches gather for a huge picnic. Each family brings a covered dish—everything from crunchy fried chicken and homemade biscuits to creamy banana pudding and fruit cobblers. The tradition got its unusual name during the pioneer days when the feast was spread out on large quilts. These days tables are usually set up in a nearby clearing. The minister might preach a short sermon or simply lead his congregation in giving thanks before the meal. Since these dinners are usually held on a Saturday, some churches use this time to spruce up their sanctuary or cemetery. Others just enjoy the fellowship with friends and neighbors.

Charlotte Deskins
Grundy, Virginia

At the Seashore

Children pay no heed to a billowy roar
As they frolic on the calm, tranquil shore.
They wade and bathe, they swim and play,
They enjoy the ocean's foam and spray.
Seen here and there are mounds of sand,
Each planned and shaped by a tiny hand;
Little pails and shovels are left nearby
As stranger things catch the builder's eye.

As they go hunting on a sandy beach,
Eager hands stretch forth and try to reach
Treasures which the sea has left behind
For those on the land to seek and find.
How eerie are wonders bountiful to see—
Scenes presented by a barren sea—
As above the seagulls whirl and soar
When all is serene at the seashore.

P.F. Freeman

Down on the beach when the tide is out,
Beautiful things lie about—
Rubies and diamonds, shells and pearls;
Starfish, oysters, mermaids' curls;
Slabs of marble cut in sand,
Veined and smoothed, polished by hand;
Whipped-up foam I think must be
What mermaids use for cream in tea.

These and a million treasures I know
Strew the beach when the tide is low,
But very few people seem to care
For these gems scattered everywhere.
Lots of these I hide away
In an old box I found one day.
And if a beggar asks me for bread,
I will give him diamonds instead.

Mary Dixon Thayer

Beside the sea the children go
With naked feet across the sand.
The little waves run laughing so,
To try and kiss them where they stand.
They build fine houses of rainbow shells,
They dig in the sand the deepest of wells;
But always and ever, alackaday!
The waves wash their houses and wells away.

Photo from H. Armstrong Roberts

Above the sea the sun is red,
A ruby rose with heart of gold.
The clouds go floating overhead
To wrap themselves in purple fold
While we build our castles of rainbow hue,
We who are old, as the small children do;
But always and ever, alackaday!
They sink with the sun in the waves away.

Beneath the sea, do you suppose
Those maids with seaweed for their hair,
Whose feet have fins in place of toes,
Play in the houses fashioned fair,
Of dreamings and fancies and rainbow dyes,
Of sand and of shells and of sunset skies?
That this is the reason, alackaday!
The waves wash our houses and dreams away?

Harriet F. Blodgett

Vacation Memories

I know a little cottage
    Where morning glory vines
Climb on the doors and windows
    In the good old summertime.

There's an orchard by the meadow
    With a gate for you and me,
Where the apples fall, delicious,
    Underneath the apple tree.

There's a pathway to the garden;
    And I rather like the way
The roses spread their fragrance
    On a sunny summer day.

Yes, my favorite kind of cottage
    Is this little cot of mine
Where I spend two weeks' vacation
    In the good old summertime.

Verna Sparks

Let me remember moonlight on still water,
A breeze from forest fresh with scent of pine,
The warm red glow of campfire dancing brightly,
And, when the night grows cold, your hand in mine.

Let me remember quiet conversation,
Soft fire-reflected lovelight in your eyes,
The afterglow of campfire embers dying,
Then sleep at last beneath star-spangled skies.

Carol Bessent Hayman

Lazy Holiday

I know a place for fishing
Where the "big ones" like to run,
A spot where weeping willows
Keep off the summer sun.

You don't need fancy fishing rods
Or a lot of expensive bait,
Just a bamboo pole, a tin of worms,
And time to meditate.

When the birds are singing overhead
And wild flowers scent the air,
When there's a gentle zephyr
And woodland sounds are everywhere,

'Tis then that life is perfect
And troubles fade away,
A time for spinning daydreams,
On a lazy holiday.

Shirley Sallay

Old~Fashioned Picnic

Let's have an old-time picnic fest
With crock-cooled lemonade
And benches made of planks and tiles
Arranged beneath the shade.

Let's have a granite roasting pan
Of chicken, golden brown,
And heaped-up bowls of cabbage slaw,
Enough to feed the town.

Let's have some after-dinner fun
Where men and boys play ball,
Where women visit, children race,
And joy is shared by all.

Let's have a horseshoe course laid out
Where all may show their skill,
And then, before we leave for home,
There's one more pleasure still!

Homemade ice cream, hand-cranked at that,
And oh, so cool and sweet,
Will team up with grand cakes and pies
To make a special treat.

Craig E. Sathoff

Old-Fashioned Picnic

Southern Fried Chicken
Makes 8 servings

1 cup flour
½ teaspoon salt
½ teaspoon pepper
1 cup milk
2 eggs
2 3½-pound chickens, cut into serving pieces
   Peanut oil

Combine flour, salt, pepper, milk, and eggs; mix well. Dip chicken pieces in batter; set aside. Pour oil into a heavy skillet to a depth of 1 inch. Heat oil over medium heat to 350°. Gently place chicken skin-side down in skillet. Turn pieces as chicken begins to brown. When all pieces are lightly browned, reduce heat and cover. Cook for 25 to 30 minutes. Uncover and cook 10 to 15 minutes more or until large pieces are easily pierced with a fork. Drain chicken on paper towels.

Summer Fruit Pie
Makes 6 servings

¾ cup crushed graham crackers
2 tablespoons margarine, melted
1 teaspoon sugar
2 tablespoons apple jelly
1 tablespoon water
½ cup grapes
½ cup blueberries
½ cup strawberries, halved
2 fresh peaches, sliced

Preheat oven to 350°. In a bowl, stir together graham crackers, margarine, and sugar until well blended. Press crumb mixture into an 8-inch pie pan. Bake for 10 minutes. In a small saucepan, combine jelly and water. Stir over low heat for 3 minutes. Arrange fruit over baked crust. Drizzle jelly mixture over fruit. Serve either chilled or at room temperature.

Picnic Bean Pot
Makes 8 to 10 servings

1 pound dried beans (kidney, Navy, lima, or a combination), picked over
1 large onion, chopped
1 green pepper, chopped
2 tablespoons vegetable oil
¼ pound bacon
2 teaspoons salt
1 1-pound can tomatoes
2 tablespoons brown sugar
2 teaspoons prepared mustard
   Dash Tabasco sauce
½ teaspoon Worcestershire sauce

Place beans in a large saucepan, cover generously with water. Bring to a boil, reduce heat and cover. Simmer about 1 hour. In a small skillet, sauté onion and green pepper in oil for 5 minutes. Add with remaining ingredients to beans. Cover and simmer 1 hour more. Stir frequently. Add water, if needed, during cooking. This dish can be reheated over a grill or outdoor campfire before serving. May be prepared ahead and refrigerated. Reheat to serve.

Coleslaw
Makes 8 servings

1 large head cabbage, shredded
1 cup shredded red cabbage, optional
1 large carrot, grated, optional
1 medium onion, diced
3 tablespoons wine vinegar
1 tablespoon sugar
¾ cup mayonnaise
   Salt, pepper, and garlic powder

Combine cabbage, carrot, and onion in a large mixing bowl. Combine vinegar, sugar, and mayonnaise in a small bowl. Pour mayonnaise mixture over vegetables; toss. Season with salt, pepper, and garlic powder to taste. Cover and refrigerate for 2 hours before serving.

Firefly Stars

Do you recall warm nights in June
When peepers chirped a festive tune,
When grown-ups chatted on the grass
As they watched playful children pass?

Small fireflies flickered in the sky;
They winked and blinked as they passed by.
Oh, we were young and so carefree—
All full of childish fun and glee.

The fireflies led a merry chase;
We ran and leaped about the place,
Snatched tiny lanterns from the air
When they glowed brightly here and there.

We quickly popped them in a jar,
Where each one was a lively star
That twinkled in the summer night
And made a friendly bedtime light.

Louise Pugh Corder

Nighttime Country Sounds

When the evening starts to darken
And the moon begins to rise
With its golden hues a-rippling
Across the cloudless skies,
It is then I enjoy sitting
On the old veranda here,
As I listen to the night sounds
That echo far and near.

I hear a barking dog somewhere;
An owl calls from a tree.
On yonder hill a whippoorwill
Sings so melodiously.
Down back amidst the darkened woods,
On banks of country pond,
I hear the bullfrog chanting
His loud bass fiddle song.

When the summer evening darkens
And the golden moon appears,
When the daytime sounds are silenced
And the hush of night draws near,
On our old farmhouse veranda
Where the roses sweet abound,
It is there I pause and listen
To the nighttime country sounds.

Loise Pinkerton Fritz

Countryside Splendors

Green fields of sweet clover,
Gold promise of grain;
Bright sunshine and breezes,
Quick, warm drops of rain.

Clear pools of soft water,
Dark green shady nooks;
Fat honeybees scouting
By cool, bubbling brooks.

Wild flowers reach skyward;
Birds' cheery songs ring.
Sheep lie in green pastures;
Cows graze by the spring.

Nature knocks at your door
With treasures galore;
Cherished splendors abound
The countryside round.

Elisabeth Weaver Winstead

ERIK AND DANDELION

Photo Opposite
DAISY FIELD
H. Armstrong Roberts

Reflections on a Summer's Eve

Summer's twilight descends like a soft gossamer curtain drawn gently between the blaze of day and the dark of night. The children, ever mindful of their reprieve from schooltime bed schedules, slip into the cool of the evening for one more game of hide-and-seek.

And then the magic appears. Fireflies. Their twinkling lights dot the landscape like miniature candles. It is a precious beauty to behold—those sudden bursts of sparkling light against a darkening sky.

The children remember from summers past the sport of capturing these brilliant beauties.

"Fireflies!" they shout almost in unison. "Let's catch them!"

There is a scramble to find just the right jar for their captives.

"Not too big a jar," one cautions, "and not too small, either."

"And one with a lid we can punch holes in so they can breathe," says the other.

Once the jar is selected and the holes are punched, small amounts of grass and twigs are collected for the bottom of the jar. "To make a soft landing place," one child announces.

Then the hunt is on. Each child hurries to catch the evening's first firefly. The children stretch, bend, run, and jump to capture those ever-moving glimmering lights.

At last a triumphant voice cries out, "I've got one! I've got a firefly!"

The firefly, lovingly cradled in small hands, is guided ever so gently into the waiting jar. One by one it is joined by fellow fireflies until the jar is a virtual lantern of twinkling light.

Even the grown-ups, remembering their own youths, enjoy this summer pastime, an activity surely as old as time itself.

"Look, you just missed that one!" a voice calls out. "Try again!"

"Oh, good, you got it that time!" another encourages.

Everyone is caught up in the immediacy of the hunt. There is only the here and now;

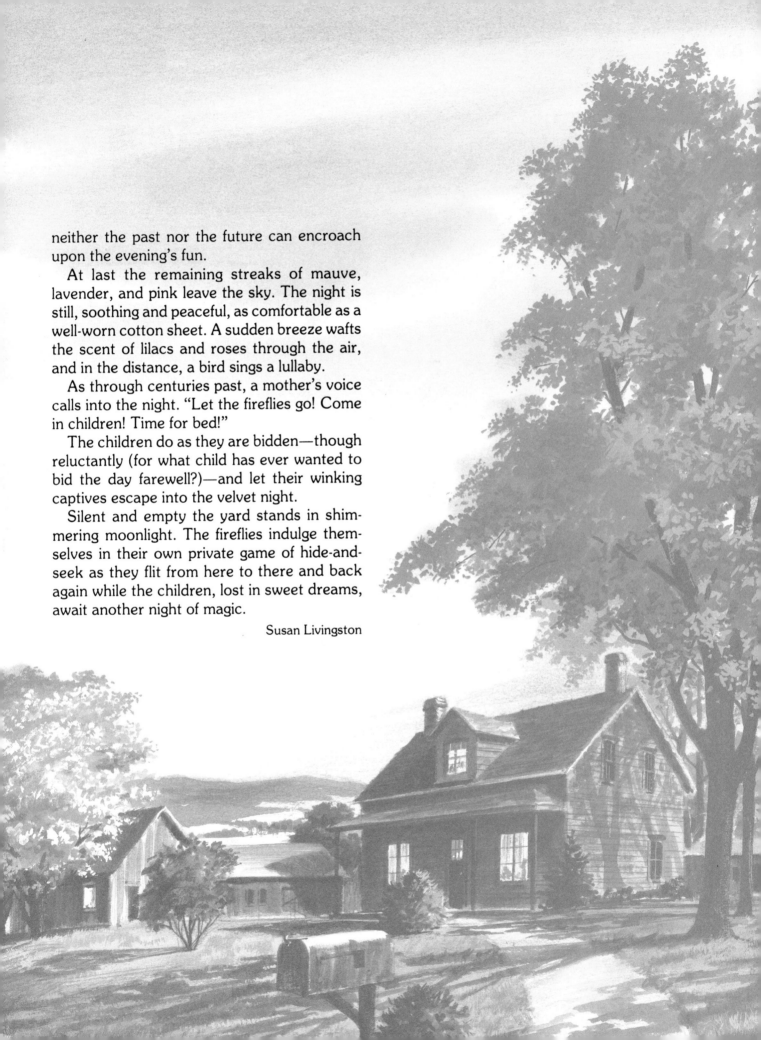

neither the past nor the future can encroach upon the evening's fun.

At last the remaining streaks of mauve, lavender, and pink leave the sky. The night is still, soothing and peaceful, as comfortable as a well-worn cotton sheet. A sudden breeze wafts the scent of lilacs and roses through the air, and in the distance, a bird sings a lullaby.

As through centuries past, a mother's voice calls into the night. "Let the fireflies go! Come in children! Time for bed!"

The children do as they are bidden—though reluctantly (for what child has ever wanted to bid the day farewell?)—and let their winking captives escape into the velvet night.

Silent and empty the yard stands in shimmering moonlight. The fireflies indulge themselves in their own private game of hide-and-seek as they flit from here to there and back again while the children, lost in sweet dreams, await another night of magic.

Susan Livingston

America

She lies between two oceans;
She boasts of mountains high.
Rich woodlands dot her landscape
While rivers flow nearby.
She offers grassy prairies
With gently rolling hills;
There's fertile soil for farming
And busy textile mills.
Her people have a birthright
That not all lands can boast...
Yes, freedom is her motto;
It's heard from coast to coast.
Though men fought hard to gain her,
This country that we love,
She's been from the beginning
A gift from God above.
Her red-striped flag waves proudly
With one star for each state;
Liberty and compassion
Are what have made her great.
Let's never take for granted
This land that is so blest;
May each of us pray for her
And give to her our best.

Marie A. Florian

Voice of America

I am the cornfields of the Middle West,
Rustling and whispering in the prairie breeze—
The snowcapped Rockies pointing to the sky.
I am youth's ambitions, symbols of these:

The cottonfields and bluegrass of the South
That stand for gracious hospitality;
The spirit of undefeated statehood
And antebellum aristocracy.

I am the rolling voice of crested waves,
Inviting all within my golden gate;
The vast Pacific of the vibrant West,
With shore and climate sure to captivate.

I am America! Its eastern towns,
Its rocky hillsides and its winding streams,
With torch to light the pathway to their dreams!

I am the cities...New York, Chicago,
All magic towns of our wondrous nation;
I am the flag that proudly waves aloft
For freedom and its commemoration.

Stella Craft Tremble

American Gateway

When I cross the blue Potomac
And see the red sun rise,
Washington portrays a glory
With marble-bordered skies.

Brave, beloved Americana,
A torch to light the past;
Jefferson's and Lincoln's faces...
Their aims to keep steadfast.

Here I come into the future
And feel the hopes of man;
Peace for hearts in harried nations,
Far planet realms to span.

When I cross the starred Potomac
As lamps turn sparkle-gay,
Freedom says an evening blessing
Upon a gold bouquet!

Inez Franck

Heritage of the Eagle

Where craggy peaks pierce azure sky
With somber hew, and regal,
In lonely lands where winds brood and sigh
Abides the majestic eagle.

Oh, splendid bird of fierce attire,
I see you in graceful silhouette,
Spread-winged and circling ever higher
In a sky-born pirouette.

You wander far from your Alpine home
To a distant timberline,
Fulfilling an innate need to roam
Like a lonely peregrine.

Your aerie lies on a lofty perch
In a mountain wilderness.
You survey your realm in keen-eyed search
And plunge for prey through emptiness.

O could I but emulate your courage...
Your fearless pursuit of aim,
Accepting life through storm or calm
With nobleness of frame.

Claire Hupe Burnham

BALD EAGLE
H. Armstrong Roberts

The Famed Red, White, and Blue

It stirs my heart when'er I see
The flag wave in the breeze.
This flag unfurled tells all the world
Of our sweet liberty,
A liberty of costly price
That others might live free.
It stirs my heart and brings a tear
When'er the flag I see.

It stirs my soul when'er I see
The famed red, white, and blue
With stars that represent each state;
It thrills me through and through!
Wherever the spot that it might wave,
In climate cold or hot,
For precious freedom we enjoy
I give my thanks to God.

Loise Pinkerton Fritz

The Flag

The wings of the ships that sail the sky
And the vessels that cruise the seas,
The tramp of feet where long armies come
And the wind in the singing trees,
The odor that comes from soil, new-turned,
The hum of machinery's wheel,
A soldier's blood and a woman's faith,
Courage and dreams and steel....

Out of their warp the flag is made,
Out of their web there comes
The banner that floats when brave men march
To the tune of the martial drums.
May we have the strength to keep it high,
God, let no dull threads mar
The flag of a thousand victories;
Keep it a guiding star.

Helen Welshimer

Statue of Liberty

The mighty woman gazes out to sea
With graceful poise and dignity.
In flowing robes and beauty crowned,
She lifts her torch of liberty.

Her kindly eyes command the view
Of wind-tossed waves that touch the shore,
And shafts of light pierce through the mist—
Her lamp of hope at freedom's door.

From high atop her pedestal,
Her form becomes a welcome sight
To all the tired and homeless souls
Who yearn to know a world more bright.

A symbol of a thriving land
Endowed with peace and liberty,
The mighty woman lifts her lamp
And silently looks out to sea.

Joy Belle Burgess

TALL SHIPS, Joe Viesti

THE STATUE OF LIBERTY, The Photo Source

I Love America

I love America for manifold
Inspiring beauty in her vast domain;
Hill, lake, woodland, prairie, desert, shore,
Blue-haloed mountain, valley, stream, and plain.

I love America for Pilgrim faith,
The firm foundation of democracy.
I love America for patriots
Who lived and died to keep their homeland free.

I love America for cherishing
Both Puritans and gallant cavaliers.
I love America for hardihood
And hope, personified by pioneers.

I love America for fostering
True freedom's first pure breath that earth might see
What untold wonders can be wrought when man
Lives unemcumbered by old tyranny.

I love America for many bloods,
Now blended into one...American.
I love America for guarding well
Her sacred trust, the rights God granted me.

I love America for all that she
Has been, and is, and yet may hope to be.
I love America for standing now...
The world's lone citadel of liberty.

Gail Brook Burket

This I Believe

I believe in the miracle of America...
In the common purpose of her people,
Their common hope and their common devotion.
My faith evades definition,
But it is built on Plymouth Rock,
Concord Bridge, and Valley Forge.

I reaffirm my faith, thinking of women and children
In covered wagons along the Oregon Trail,
Men on foot over Cumberland Gap;
How corruption and dishonor have always been answered
By high-hearted patriots.
Their blood runs strong in us,
A lasting part of what we are.

I have faith in the great dream of my country,
Bred to liberty at Runnymede and nourished
By three centuries of unselfish devotion.
I believe that America is on the verge
Of something noble...
On the border of a new glory that shall shine
In the lives of all people everywhere.
This I believe.

Helen Virden

THE LIBERTY BELL

High aloft inside the steeple
Hung a strong and rugged bell;
Below, the Continental Congress
Spoke of war—and peace, as well.

They discussed unfair taxation,
Trade restrictions, and the plea
Of unrepresented people
Quite determined to be free.

A plan for life and liberty
And happiness each one pursues
Was adopted by the Congress,
Then the bell rang out the news.

Yes, it proclaimed a declaration
For the freedom of this land;
In its song for independence,
Its clanging music sounded grand.

It is cherished as a symbol
Of the freedom we hold dear,
And its very presence echoes
The happy news of yesteryear.

Billie McCoy

Blessings of Liberty

The Declaration of Independence proclaimed our separation from England, and the Articles of Confederation which followed were designed only to set up among the states a "firm league of friendship with each other." By 1787, problems had arisen which demonstrated that the Articles placed no authority in a central government. The members of the Continental Congress met in May, but they were sanctioned for "the sole and express purpose of revising the Articles of Confederation." Those who came to Philadelphia, however, were of two beliefs: those who wanted to retain the rights of the states and those who wanted a strong central government. A compromise had to be reached. That compromise became the Constitution of the United States.

Its Preamble inspires awe as it sets the tone and states the reasons for the Constitution's existence:

We the People of the United States,
Here is an affirmation that the inhabitants of the land, through their elected representatives, speak as one, not as thirteen individual states.

in Order to form a more perfect Union,
This is the clarion which abolished the "league of friendship" of the Articles and set up a strong government for a single nation.

establish Justice,
A strong central government, however, will never forget that its first duty is to the justice of the individual, to "We the people."

insure domestic Tranquility,
As a "man's home is his castle," so this country will provide for its citizens a haven within its borders.

provide for the common defence,
This document provides protection for its people from enemies both without and within its borders.

promote the general Welfare,
This new government embraced the responsibility for the well-being of all its citizens.

and secure the Blessings of Liberty
Perhaps the most beautiful phrase in this document, especially to those who have ever lived or travelled abroad.

to ourselves and our Posterity,
How thankful we are that those far-sighted men of 1787 included us in their dreams!

do ordain and establish this Constitution for the United States of America.
These courageous and confident words created the greatest document since the *Magna Carta* and invested it with the authority to stand as the foundation for a sovereign nation.

After 200 years, we may forget the circumstances leading up to the Constitutional Convention. We may forget the men who argued the matter of states' rights versus a central government. We may even forget the men who framed this document and set down its words.

But we cannot forget the "blessings of liberty." We cannot forget the justice, domestic tranquility, and common defense provided for our general welfare by the Constitution.

And we cannot forget that what happened in the city of Philadelphia during the hot summer of 1787 makes us some of the most fortunate people on the face of the earth.

For this, we thank the delegates of the Convention of 1787.

For this, we thank God.

The Climb

There's a beautiful view at the top of the hill,
If the will be yours to climb.
There's always a lift and a rift in the clouds
To disclose the peaks sublime.
The road may be rough,
You may blow and puff;
But never you mind, you'll be scaling the bluff,
Then yours is the view at the top of the hill,
If you've but the will to climb.

James McGregor Beatty

Sharing

Let not your dream remain a dream
Forever in your mind,
Kept to yourself, a glowing gleam,
By others undivined.
Clothe it with reality;
Give it vesture, worth.
Let it carry melody
Along the streets of earth,
In shop and field to kindle song
Within the hearts of men;
And some who have been silent long
Shall find their voices again.

Isabel M. Wood

Pioneer Paths

I like to think that they who came
And made their homes the first,
Looked out upon these sunlit fields
And quenched their want and thirst.

They saw these skies with hallowed love
And handed down the plan
To build our strength, to plant our faith,
And thank the God of man.

I like to think they wove their songs
Beside the early fires;
They heard the copper kettles hum
And felt their hearts' desires.

They blessed the freedom that we know,
The peace of pine-green hills;
They made us glad to carry on
The virtue of their wills.

I like to think they beat the paths
That lead us here today;
They saw the roses growing wild,
The beavers at their play.

This was the place where dreams would live
And doors would open wide;
In all the milestones we reach,
Their hopes are satisfied.

Inez Franck

The Pioneer

Of all the heroes we hold dear,
One stands alone—the pioneer.
He traveled west, but not for fame;
No throng was there to shriek his name.
He faced wild beast with steady gun;
His song arose to greet the sun.
He felled the trees in swampy wood,
Grubbed rock and root to plant his food.

He lived with nature...felt that man
Should carry out the God-formed plan
Of breaking fallow ground and loam
For basic need of hearth and home.
The star of liberty shone bright
To light his pathway in the night;
His freedom gained through storm and blast
We now inherit from the past.

Through rain and shine, a higher view
Gave him the courage to subdue
A love of ease. He gained control
Of mind and body, heart and soul.
Give us his vision as we press
On through today's wilderness...
Give us the courage now and here
Of our ancestral pioneer.

Stella Craft Tremble

The Trail West

Golden dust still shifts and spirals
Along this well-worn way,
When zephyrs with their gentle
    stirring
Sing of a bygone day,
When creaking wheels carved this
    trail
Through sod and tufted grass
And left their deep-worn ruts to
    show
Where stalwart souls had passed.

Paintings by John Slobodnik

Pioneers with hope and courage,
Who gazed off toward the west,
Blazed their path across the
    prairie
And withstood each bitter test.
Forgers of a trail and nation
Endured the hardships of the
    plain,
Crossed streams and snow-filled
    passes
Till the west was won by wagon
    trains.

Golden dust still shifts and spirals
Along this well-worn way,
Where ox shoes now lie buried deep
In the tramplings of a bygone day.
And when the singing wind
    sweeps by
And ripples through the prairie
    grass,
The old trail west still faintly
    hears
Wayside echoes of the silent past.

Joy Belle Burgess

Lilacs
on the Prairie

She packed a lilac root among her things
And tended it with pride along the way,
That it might thrive and grow for many springs
Against her cabin door, rough-hewn and gray.

A background for a wild bird's airy song
She visioned it; a fragrant cooling shade
From western sun that wearied the slow throng
Of pioneers who moved on unafraid.

The cabin in which she lived is now gone,
But solemn travelers passing by the way
See lilac buds unfolding on the lawn,
And know a woman dwelled, serene and gay.
For here is beauty that she planted well—
A monument as, yearly, small buds swell.

LaVerna Hassler

Women of the Plains

She owned a great grandfather's clock
That stood behind the door
To name the virgin hours
Time had not kept before.

She made her tallow candles
To send a trembling flame
Against the dark wilderness
Her family must tame.

A warming box for glowing coals
Brought from a neighbor's hearth,
An iron plow, rough and strong,
To break the prairie earth.

An unlatched door for strangers,
A cabin filled with fears,
Hollowed from the wilderness...
High-hearted pioneers.

Helen Virden

Photo Overleaf
LOG CABIN WITH GARDEN
Ken Dequaine

Domain

They little dreamt that time would write their names
With pride and honor in the hall of fame.
Their recompense for weeks of weary toil,
Preparing one small hopeful patch of soil,
Was sprouting seed which greened and grew, until
At last the treasured heads began to fill
With gold for daily bread and next year's seed.
Of each small kernel there was urgent need.
In spite of hardships, plague and drought and flood,
Their work was not in vain; they found life good,
Rejoicing in each growing plot of grain
And thanking God for seed and soil and rain.

Far wider than the scopes of wildest dreams,
Which sometimes glow with strange, prophetic gleams,
Are those vast seas of wheat on prairie plain,
Whose source goes back to pioneer domain.

Rosa Mary Clausen-Mohr

Emigrant Trail

Who says their ancient footprints now are gone
From off the desert floor and mountainside?
And who can say the ruts from wagon wheels
Have left no record of their fateful ride?

Each year the sands have shifted restlessly
To paint new landscapes framed by sea and sky,
While melting snows have etched the mountainside
And carved designs where verdant valleys lie...
Cascaded by the springtime freshet's plan
To shape new paths and gullies of its own.

But through it all, the marks are ever there,
Imprinted by an ancient boot, hand-sewn
And built to match the grim determined stride
That dared to leave it sculptured in the sod!

Ben Sweeney

City Dweller

My spirit longs for open fields,
For wide old furrows wet and brown;
And yet I live and move and breathe
In cramped places of the town
And work my little round of days
Held in the city's crowded ways.

Yet here I have a window box,
Where mignonette and pansies grow.
I summerfallow with a fork
And use a ladle for a hoe.
I bought a root of sage to see
If it would really grow for me.

I shut my eyes and smell the breath
Of warm, wet sod where sunshine lies
And see again the fields of home
Beneath the sweep of prairie skies,
Spring breaking o'er the lonely plain,
The welcome coming of the rain.

And yet, my tiny window box
Brings comfort to my homesick heart,
A little plant of living green
Makes me somehow a vital part
Of all the world's wide breadth and span,
Kin of the nationhood of man.

Edna Jaques

Photo Opposite
GOLDEN GATE
Ed Cooper

The Country Inside

It is one of those brassy hot days when the sky stares back at you unblinking and blue. My hoe handle shines with a hand-rubbed patina, veteran of many plantings and harvests. At my feet, exposed worms wriggle and thrash, anxious to return to their cool subterranean homes. The dirt smells wonderful, rich and fertile.

I stop my hoeing for a moment to study the others around me. Mr. Olson, over there, carefully sifts the peat moss into his symmetrical hills of soil, preparing them to receive Burpee's Best Burpless Beauties. His hands caress the earth like a lover's, and he whistles a tuneless melody to no one in particular. On any other day, Mr. Olson would be consulting with subcontractors or examining airplane fuselages, but not today. Today is Saturday, and Mr. Olson is a tiller of the earth.

Six furrows over, Ms. Fletcher stakes her tomato seedlings, regaling them with images of

tall and stately tomato plants dripping with ruby fruit. Ms. Fletcher is a sociologist and recently read an article about communicating with the vegetable world or some such. In any case, she is giving those baby tomatoes her best shot.

Behind me, Mr. and Mrs. Abrams argue about the proper care and feeding of his sweet corn plants; she being an advocate of steer manure and he of chemical fertilizers. The plants stand, unimpressed, drinking in the hot sun and nodding sagely now and then.

A bit further away, a little boy pats the soil over his pumpkin seeds, whispering what must be an incantation guaranteed to inspire the hugest jack-o-lantern ever.

All around, folks dig and weed and speculate on such natural phenomena as rain and dew and snails and slugs. It is a great place to be on a sun-filled Saturday morning.

The plot of ground we all share is small really, by Kansas or Iowa standards—even by Southern California standards. We don't care. Dirt is rare in Los Angeles. Oh, we have smog and dust and sand and other sophisticated kinds of stuff, but not much real honest-to-goodness dirt. This particular patch of it is located in the triangular area created by the intersection of three freeways. For a small fee you can rent a piece of the plot and plant whatever you like—flowers, herbs, vegetables, whatever. These farmers read their seed catalogs in condos and townhouses, then come here to their little triangular countryside to place their offerings in Mother Earth. And what is so fantastic is that things actually grow! Right here in the big city. There are no golden waves of grain or fluffy fields of cotton bolls bursting with whiteness, but we have a delightful assortment of leaves and vines and blossoms and berries.

Something about the dirt and digging makes everyone equal out here. It doesn't matter if you have a Ph.D. in metalurgical engineering—if your peas don't come up, you are eligible for sympathy and advice. "Say, Phil, did you try coffee grounds? I hear they work wonders for your PH balance."

Here you can forget the office, the board meetings, the patients clamoring in the waiting room. Here you do what you can, then you sit back and watch with something akin to awe as the water and the sun and God do the rest. It is humbling, and very reassuring, to know things are in good hands after all.

On your knees in the dirt, life's problems are reduced to quack grass and dandelions. You pull them out, shake off their hairy little roots and toss them in the trash. You feel like you have truly accomplished something. It isn't like trends and stock futures or nebulous little viruses that refuse to be pinned down. Out here, if you have snails, you get snail bait. It's that simple.

Then there are the tangible rewards. Nothing compares to dragging home a basket of sweet, juicy tomatoes, still warm from the sun, or a bag full of bright green peas, or an armload of corn with silky tassels waving victoriously. These trophies are truly glorious. "Yes, I grew them myself," you answer modestly when the company remarks on their freshness.

The act of cultivation brings out the neighborliness in folks, too. "How are those potatoes doing this year?" "Say, did you hear what happened to Sam's cabbages?" "Put some marigolds around your tomatoes next year, Helene—keeps the slugs away." A garden is a friendly place, full of honesty and fresh air and smiles.

I guess it's not so much the countryside I witness here as it is the *country-inside*—the part of us that yearns for simplicity and basics, that longs for clear-cut goals and concrete achievements. We may not be aware of it at first, for sometimes it takes a little sun, some soil, and a bit of sweat to bring it out. With some tending, however, the part of each of us that belongs to the earth begins to flourish, just like the seedlings at my feet. Smiling, I turn my back to the sun and bury my hoe in the earth once more, gently urging my infant crops to grow.

Pamela Kennedy

Song of Appalachia

Appalachia, I hear your song—
Borne on the wayward breeze
And in the murmur of trees,
In the river's rollicking tune
And the cardinal's nesting croon.

Appalachia, I hear your song—
In the wheels of moving trains
And the soft tap of summer rains,
In the highway's hurrying teem
And murmur of the mountain stream.

Appalachia, I hear your song—
In the city's busy rush
And scamper of squirrels in the brush,
In the call of geese southward bound
And baying of the hunting hound.

Appalachia, I hear your song—
In young voices that sing at school,
Learning about the Golden Rule,
In hum of bees in a clover field
And rustle of corn at harvest's yield.

Appalachia, I hear your song—
In the drone of streaking jets on high
And the roar of trains rolling by,
In the feet of deer rustling leaves
And coo of pigeons in the eaves.

Appalachia, I hear your song—
In choristers singing in the church
And vesper sparrows in the birch;
In every season all year through,
Appalachia, I will sing of you!

Amanda Meade Thompson

Sweet Summer

Across the rolling hills,
Like waves on summer seas,
I see the prairie grasses
Waving in the breeze.
The dawning day to greet,
A meadowlark is singing
In whistled love-notes sweet,
   "Summer—sweet summer."

Above the snowy cloud-ships
Across the blue skies go,
Their shadows falling on the grass,
Where hidden far below
A little bird is warming eggs
'Neath a yellow breast
And happily is listening to
One song from all the rest,
   "Summer—sweet summer."

Oh, happy were we children
When we used to play,
Racing o'er rolling hills
All the livelong day.
Oh, beauty bird, with magic voice,
As then, my heart would hear
Your whistled notes at early morn,
Your love song to your dear,
   "Summer—sweet summer."

Mabel Smith Shepard

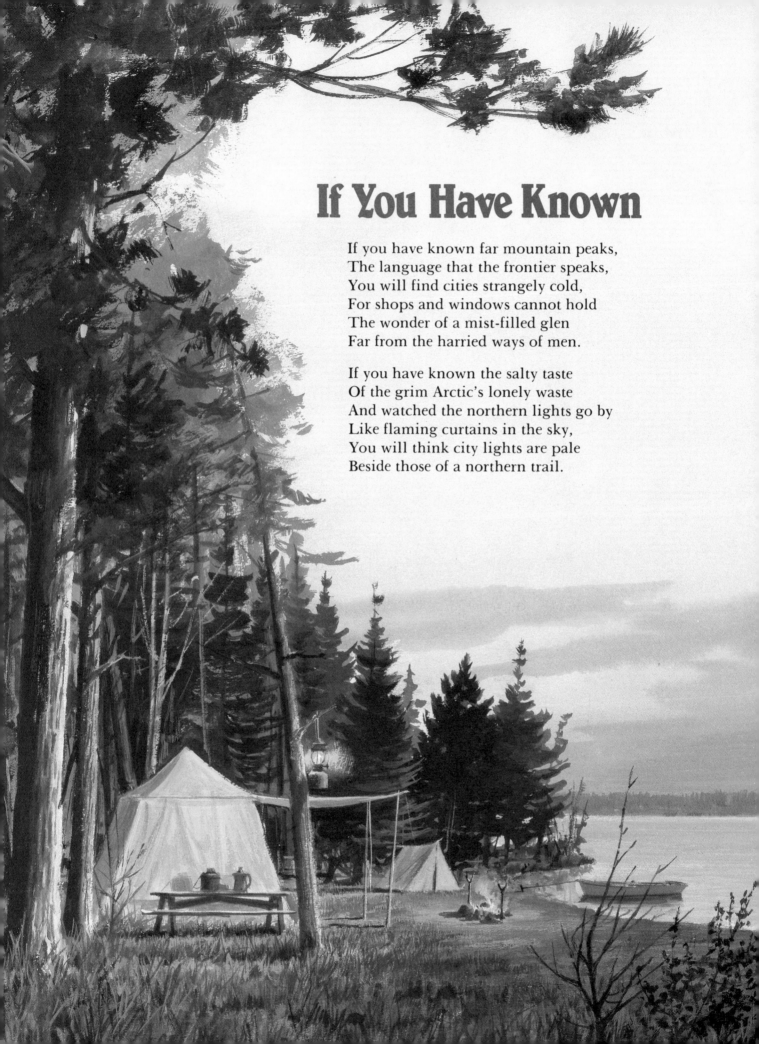

If You Have Known

If you have known far mountain peaks,
The language that the frontier speaks,
You will find cities strangely cold,
For shops and windows cannot hold
The wonder of a mist-filled glen
Far from the harried ways of men.

If you have known the salty taste
Of the grim Arctic's lonely waste
And watched the northern lights go by
Like flaming curtains in the sky,
You will think city lights are pale
Beside those of a northern trail.

If you have earned a living where
At your back door, tall mountains rear
White-crested peaks against the sky,
Or heard a wounded cougar cry,
Your heart will never settle down
To living in a little town.

If you have slept where campfires glow,
Surrounded by dark trees and snow,
And watched the sunrise, stark and cold,
Roll up o'er valleys bright as gold,
You will be kin of all who dare
The lonely trails to God-knows-where.

                    Edna Jaques

Sunrise at Grand Canyon

In dimness of a quarter moon
The nearby cliffs are seen,
Worn fragments of the ages past
Gripping bits of green.

Across the starry canvas sweeps
A master artist's brush,
Leaving in the darkened sky
The faintest rosy blush.

Crimson hues are deepening;
The painter's brush is bold
And streaks the canvas in the east
With fiery red and gold.

Finally, from out of the mist,
Rise peaks of calico,
And jagged cliffs stand tall above
The river far below.

Beatrice Branch

Photo Opposite
THE GRAND CANYON
Ed Cooper

Moods of the Sea

Sparkling and splashing and rippling,
Tossing the foam in their glee,
Blue as the heavens above them
Are the dancing waves of the sea.

Swiftly advancing, receding,
Washing the glittering strands,
The billowy sea is rolling,
Lapping the sun-kissed sands.

Over the deep, briny waters,
Calm as an ocean can be,
The waves are plainly revealing
The happy mood of the sea.

But suddenly, out in the distance,
The waters grow leaden and gray;
The whitecaps are bobbling and bouncing,
And gone is the brightness of day.

Howling in violent fury,
Breaking with noisy roar,
Billows leap angrily skyward,
Far up on the rocky shore.

Tumbling in boisterous fashion,
Wrathfully tossing the spray,
The waves, now so powerful and cruel,
The ocean's temper betray.

Ebbing and flowing forever,
Peaceful or wild as may be,
There is never a quiet moment
For the busy tides of the sea.

Restless, rebellious, bewitching,
Whatever the mood of the tide,
How mighty and great is the ocean,
How powerless man by its side.

Agnes Davenport Bond

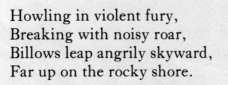

Vacation Surprise

A magic time when distant spots
Possess a lovely glow;
A time when hearts gain wanderlust
To fly where trade winds blow.

The winding trail, the lush green forests,
The sand, the sea of blue
Offer fun beyond your dreams,
Adventures bright and new.

A quiet farm with rolling fields,
The camp with gear and tent,
A crystal stream with fishing joys
Are beauties heaven-sent.

Vacation is a magic time
With wonders to behold,
Happy holidays for you
As all your dreams unfold.

Enjoy the golden hours
Wherever you may roam,
But you will find, to your surprise,
You're glad to get back home.

LaVerne P. Larson

Photo Overleaf
GOAT BEACH, CALIFORNIA
Ed Cooper

No Need

No need to travel tiresome miles;
Just stand in your back door—
See the visions waiting there,
Scenes you've never noticed before.

Long greening hills, a mountaintop,
A river gently flowing,
A rim of trees behind the hedge,
Where leaves are softly waving.

A homemade kite is flying high,
With tail dancing a bit;
You cannot see the sturdy cord,
Just a small boy holding it.

See the blue sky gently touch
The hilltops' greening rim
That curves into a crescent
Like a regal diadem.

No need to travel tiresome miles;
Just stand in your back door—
See the beauty waiting there,
Scenes you've never noticed before.

Mamie Ozburn Odum

Reminisce with *Nostalgia Ideals*

Do you remember the "Big Band Era?" Carousels, early automobiles, and Cripple Creek days? All these and many other scenes from the past will be explored in our next issue, *Nostalgia Ideals.*

Join us as we go back in time, and rediscover memories from your past, as does Ms. Adele Gordon of Bayville, New York, who writes:

> Received my second copy of *Ideals* and am simply thrilled with the thoughtfulness of a dear friend—and your wonderful magazine.
>
> As a senior citizen, I find many memories between these pages.

Thank you, Ms. Gordon! Why not show your thoughtfulness by sharing the beauty of *Ideals* with a friend? Or start your own subscription with our *Nostalgia* issue.

ACKNOWLEDGMENTS

CAMPER'S HONEYMOON by Carol Bessent Hayman was reprinted with permission of *MODERN BRIDE,* copyright © 1987, CBS Magazines, a division of CBS, Inc. Our sincere thanks to the following whose addresses we were unable to locate: James McGregor Beatty for THE CLIMB; Beatrice Branch for SUNRISE AT GRAND CANYON; Rosa Mary Clausen-Mohr for DOMAIN; Mary Dixon Thayer for DOWN ON THE BEACH; Inez Franck for AMERICAN GATEWAY and PIONEER PATHS; P.F. Freeman for AT THE SEASHORE; Lucy E. Russell for SUMMERTIME: Mabel Smith Shepherd for SWEET SUMMER; Amanda Meade Thompson for SONG OF APPALACHIA from *I SING OF APPALACHIA* by Amanda M. Brewer; Stella Craft Tremble for THE PIONEER and VOICE OF AMERICA; Mildred W. Phillips for THE FLAG by Helen Welshimer; and Isabel M. Wood for SHARING.